CHEZ NOUS

CHEZ NOUS

ANGIE ESTES

Oberlin College Press

http://www.oberlin.edu/ocpress

Publication of this book was supported in part by a grant from the Ohio Arts Council.

Ohio Arts Council
A STATE AGENCY
THAT SUPPORTS PUBLIC
PROGRAMS IN THE ARTS

Library of Congress Cataloging-in-Publication Data

Estes, Angie.
    Chez Nous / Angie Estes.
    (The FIELD Poetry Series v. 17)
    I. Title.   II. Series.

LC: 2004117467
ISBN: 0-932440-99-1   (pbk.)

for Kath

and in memory of
John Douglas Estes
1920–2002

I too felt in me the need of making it be a thing that could be named without using its name. After all one had known its name anything's name for so long, and so the name was not new but the thing being alive was always new.

Gertrude Stein

CONTENTS

I have sometimes thought that a woman's nature is like a great house full of rooms.

Edith Wharton

It is part of morality not to be at home in one's home.

Theodor Adorno

TRUE CONFESSIONS

If I'd been a ranch, they would've
called me the Bar Nothing.
                              Gilda, 1946

I can never get a zipper
to close. Maybe that stands
for something, what do you think?
I think glamour is its own
allure, thrashing and
flashing, a lure, a spoon
as in spooning, as in *l'amour*
in Scotland, where I once watched
the gorse-twisted hills unzip
to let a cold blue lake
between them. St. Augustine says
the reason why humans behave
as they do is because they are
not living in their true
home. In Rita Hayworth's
first film, for example, *Dante's Inferno*
is a failing Coney Island
concession, and Margarita Cansino
plays the part of Rita
Cansino playing herself. And the true
home of glamour, by which
I mean of course the grammar
of glamour, is Scotland
because *glamour* is a Scottish variant
of *grammar* with its rustle of moods
and desires. Which brings us back to
the zipper and why we want it

to close, each hook climbing another
the way words ascend a sentence, trying on
its silver suture like clothes. In a satin
strapless gown, Gilda slowly peeled off
her black arm-length gloves, showed
how to strip down, diagram a sentence: *Put
the blame on Mame, boys.* In 1946, a pin-up
of Rita Hayworth and the name *Gilda*
rode on the side of the atomic bomb
tested at Bikini Atoll; it was summer
and you could buy a record, hear the sound
of her beating heart. By her last
film, *The Wrath of God*, her hair was a burning
bush; she couldn't remember
her lines, whether it's memory or loss
we're in need of most: to remember
the way home or forget
who we are when we get there.
*Every man I have known has fallen
in love with Gilda and wakened
with me.* St. Augustine asked, *But when I love you,
what do I love?* He asked the earth
and the breeze, perfume, song,
flesh, the sun, the moon
and stars: *My question was the attention
I gave to them, and their response
was their beauty.*

PARAMOUR

An adverb by way of
love, what's par for
l'amour is par
for the course. Say
you're out for dinner one evening
with Yves, and you think of
the phrase *evening*
of life. Who doesn't want
to be called something
other than the name
we're given: the cow we call
boeuf or *beef* when eaten, the house
when it's lived in,
home, and the one we
go home with, *love.*
Lysippus, the Greek
sculptor, used to say
that his predecessors made men
as they really were, but he made them as
they appeared to be, just as Picasso
replied to those who claimed Stein
did not look like the portrait
he made: *she will.* What makes
the wine the wine, is it the grape
or the *terroir,* terror or
terrain? You think *Burgundy*
evening, assigned
age of light, first
sign of winter, art of
decay: *assignage,* the art of curing
cheese, *fromage,* what the French call
feet of the angels.

Rendez-Vous

after Bernini

She's the *crème de la crème, la crème*
de God's *cœur*, pure
as butter under the painted sky,
and He, the light falling always
from an unseen source, narrowing
in gilded shafts to pierce
her heart a second time: *l'éclair*
éclairer, flash of lightning, pastry so light
it's *pâtisserie*. No wonder St. Teresa's
in ecstasy—is it architecture, sculpture
in the round, relief? *In my Father's house*
are many mansions, the many-chambered rose
religieuse at Ladurée, which only proves
Pascal was right—that faith in God is reasonable
because revelation can be comprehended
only by faith, which is justified
by revelation. The icing of the *religieuse*
flows like the folds of a nun's
habit, her robes let loose
like the word for
peony, many-chambered world
without end, each *appoggiatura*
the opposite of apology—not amenable,
without amends, no amen.

AMUSE-BOUCHE

Bite-sized excitement for the tongue
and eye: consider which daughter
of Zeus and Mnemosyne she
might be. Think of Hansel
and Gretel leaving bits
of bread to find their way
back home, of the birds who couldn't
believe their luck. Amuse me, muse
of the mouth, mosaic,
museum with your silver
and garnet brooch—give me *bouche*
à bouche, then *brioche*, *crème Chantilly*,
high C ascending
the gothic nave of the upper
palate of Maria Callas. *All in one*
breath, she said, *is how*
bel canto should be sung
so that performed correctly you can
hear the audience hold
its breath.

    Cleopatra: *I'll set a bourn how far to be beloved.*
    Antony: *Then must thou needs find out new heaven, new earth.*

Because a little knowledge
is a dangerous thing, a little
Everest, a bit of
evidence, a little death, *le petit*
mort is a dangerous thing,
which is why Antony called Cleopatra

Egypt and not his *Rome*
away from Rome. At the end
of *Aida*, the lovers lie together at
last, their breath held
beneath the ground, but in
Act II, when the triumphant Egyptian
army returned and Callas hit
E flat, the audience had already gone
wild, beyond any
bread crumbs they might
have followed home.

ELEGY

Think of nothing so much
as light thinking of where
it will hide when all
the bulbs have gone out,
and follow Vita Sackville-West's advice
to plant flowers you can recognize
in the dark because *elegance*,
said Madame Errazuriz, *means*
elimination, a room edited
to make room for more
room so that every object stands
in relief. *I have been memorizing*
the room, Queen Christina replied; *in the future,*
in my memory, I shall live
a great deal in this room. Inviolable,
really, like the violence,
the violins in the andante of Schubert's
fourteenth string quartet, the *v* sound,
Poe claimed, is the most
beautiful of all because it is
the sound heard in violets
and viols, although I have come
to prefer the sound of *x* because it marks
the spot in *exile* and *exit*, exquisite
and exact. Before she was
Harriet Brown, Greta Garbo
was Greta Gustafsson. Once
you were here. Now you are
the most elegant of all, the future
as we imagine it
to be: a beautiful room, vacant

except for the blonde light
flooding its face, like Garbo
staring ahead at the end
of *Queen Christina*, already
thinking of nothing, no longer
needing her director's advice.

PORTRAIT

From below, the pearled bowl of sky
is perfect like the belly of a trout
unslit, a room never

entered: past tense, past
time—veins filled
entirely with blue like the milk

from ewes that ripens in the limestone
caves of Cambalou—and in that room
there is no room for

memory, smeared place like the one left
by Picasso when he wiped Stein's
face from the portrait after more than eighty

sittings, saying *I can't see you anymore
when I look*. Then he went away and
painted it, not *a capriccio*

but by heart. What's wrong with
the past is that it's never over
and over again: the irises keep opening

into *fleurs-de-lis*, and *le désir*
and *les idées* come back
each April as *des iridées*. Alma

mater, Alma Mahler, mother of
God—who left the rose in
rosary? *Earthly Paradise, Double*

Delight, Mister Lincoln (color of
the scent that rose from his
chest). *Enfleurer, enfleurage, le fromage*

des rois et le roi des fromages— Roquefort,
a glass of Hermitage, a limestone cliff: *I like
a view*, Stein said, *but I like to sit*

with my back turned to it. Like heaven,
like *truite au bleu*
on your plate, the entire blue

face of the sky has only one
eye, which never
blinks.

Kind of Blue

Because most stars were born more than six billion
years ago, the average color of the universe has changed
since that bluer period when there were more young stars.
                The Cosmic Spectrum and the Color of
                                                the Universe

So the universe is not blue
after all, not even green

but beige because the stars are
older than we thought. But is it

sad, even sadder than
we knew? Describe the sound

of doves—is it *coo coo*
coo or *who who who*? The French

would say it's *rue rue rue*
and in Italy it would be summer,

morning, already brocade,
Cecilia Bartoli gargling. And the throats

of doves, are they beautiful
or true in their blue and pink

embroidery? Young stars burn
hot and blue but those near death

are red. *Did your father believe*
in God? and the deer leaped

so high above the road I believed
it had been hit by a car. Dear falling

note, intention, dear
no more, dear rain,

give it up. What remains and need
not be mentioned we'll call

what have you, musica ficta: not
what's written down but what's

been played. What if
you paused for a minuet

instead of a minute? The dark
might sky, the blue might

star, the always
could open, the close

might earth. The doves
are just around

the corner, like a train
before it turns into

view. Miles Davis was
right: *there will be fewer*

chords but infinite possibilities
as to what to do with them. The doves

are coming, *true*
true true.

PROVERBS

Mortise and tenon, tongue and
groove, tongue-in-cheek, the tenor
holds the note until it dovetails
in air like the white kerchief of
the Holy Spirit tied around the neck
of God in Masaccio's *Trinity*, the dove
more banner than bird, which from
the beginning was the word for
verb—part sky, part earth, part
of speech expressing action, occurrence,
existence. *It is wonderful,*
Stein said, *the number of mistakes*
a verb can make. Pardon, scusi, word
for word, tell me whether the theory
holds and, if so, how we will
hold up, hold out, hold
on, and then I will hold you
to your promise the way the arms of God
hold up the cross, which holds up
Christ. *To have and to hold*: hold
that thought. *Besides being able to be*
mistaken and to make mistakes
verbs can change to look like
themselves or to look
like something else. The inscription above
the skeleton below Christ's feet, for example,
says the same holds
for you: *I was that which you are,*
and what I am you will be. So much
for *vers libre. Do you think he looks*
like himself? they asked, glancing toward

his casket. *In the hold*, in Masaccio's fresco,
>	the grave is a wall with a barrel vault
pierced through, deep chamber below
>	a coffered ceiling where God holds forth
in rose and black. *Behold,*
>	*I show you a mystery*: a ruse
is a ruse is a ruse. In Latin,
>	to have verve is to have
words. It could be a version,
>	aversion, a verse: please
advise. Not much we can know save
>	the redbud, which wears its heart
on its leaves.

CADENZA

Not the unripped stitch
of the cicada or the late September
daze, maples struck with their own
good fortune, but a falling
inflection, as at the end
of a sentence or the fall of
a melody to its final
note: the cadence
of belief, something you might
give credence to if there were
a table small enough
to hold it, might feel the tightening
of piety when it has given up
its *e*. What is the difference
between ripeness and letting time
have its way? *I would as lief*
come now as later, as *cadence*
comes from *cadenza*, from Italian
cadere, to fall. *Please*
help me, I'm falling
in love with you, the song
goes, a progression of chords moving
to a close like the fall
of Rome or love—the difference
between grapes nudging each other
quietly in Puligny-Montrachet
and those grown just over
the fence, the distance between
singing in harmony and singing
off key. Memory has its own
credenza, sideboard of belief,

no legs or credentials
but moveable by definition, as all
furniture is for the French. *Creo*
que sí, bien sûr, sur lies, as long
as cicadas tick and narcissus
inch up and bloom
by the porch, although the house
and its porch are no longer
there, like the words
you speak or the song's
refrain, like leaf rain
you don't recognize
as rain until it falls.

BADINERIE

for Gertrude Stein

Oh gloves of Sweden, you
with the suede verbs, whoever
yearns for you has more
than earned her heap of
earth and its kern and slur
of notes. How much space
should we leave between
words? Enough for Elijah
to come in or for
love to let itself
out? Let it be smooth
and limber, the *passaggio* of
the soprano's notes, like the evening
passeggiata among the sequins
of stars in her dress or the certain
stroll of perfume that makes
you remember and then
makes you forget. *Dolce vita,*
Trueste, Poème, Rendez-
vous, L'Heure bleue, Vol
de Nuit, or just a few drops of
Chanel No. 5—Marilyn Monroe claimed
that's all she needed to wear
in bed. The route of the scroll,
volute, down the Grand Canal
isn't straight or narrow—neither
Roman nor Greek—but *velouté*
all the way, and whether rowing or
riding by train, we move

forward facing forward
or back. But if what we are
swayed by is not finally
the same as what persuades
us, then how, how
now, brown noun?

CHÈRE PERSONNE,

if you were coming dressed
as *quelqu'un*, a robin riding in
her next, I'd know that spring
was over and understand the difference
between *n'est-ce pas?* and nest.
But what approaches *au prochain*
arrêt is neither stop
nor rest, but just the station Arnaud
claimed, *Je suis l'espace*
où je suis. I'm the space
where I am, *bien sûr, mais ma chère*
personne, you're nobody till
somebody loves you,
or so the song maintains, so let
the seasons sail me the way
andantes snow when Amish buggies
orbit roads, single
file in their black tilted bonnets,
bold-faced titles of what's
ahead.

for Emily Dickinson

Vis-à-Vis

Giraffe from Sennar, Paris, 1827

What is always
looking back at itself: the *s*
of the *tête-à-tête*

sofa, a kind of sleigh
for two, never slight but sleight
of hand, legerdemain,

as in light
of hand across the snow,
across the manuscript

of Verdi's duet between lovers
where the handwriting of Verdi
and the handwriting of Pepina

alternate, lie side by
side like the runners
of a sleigh in snow—

compared with the blue-black
tongue of the giraffe, which is more
silent? Her skin, stained-

glass window, each pane
opaque and leaded
with light around its edges, we call

hide, we call *stepping stones to*
heaven: Notre Dame de la Belle
Verrière, Our Lady of the Beautiful

Window, *for now we see through a glass,*
darkly. Lady-in-waiting
lying in wait but never lying

low like the law, *that which is*
set down, she was a gift
to the king of France from the viceroy

of Egypt while he waged war
on the Greeks. From the Arabic *zarafa, charming,*
lovely one, the giraffe—tallest

of animals—has the longest distance
between head and heart, but not so
long as the distance she rode

from the hills of Sennar on a camel's
back, floated on feluccas up
the Nile, sailed from Alexandria

to Marseille—standing in the hold, neck
rising through a hole in the deck—
and walked from Marseille

to Paris. *Then face to*
face, the crowds adored
her: *Here's looking at you.*

With the largest eyes
of any mammal, she's the Egyptian
hieroglyph for *foretell*: *here's looking*

at the future. *For now we see*
through a glass, darkly, looking up
the staircase in the *cabinet de curiosités*,

now known *even as also I am*
known as *le Muséum d'Histoire Naturelle*
de La Rochelle on the west coast

of France, while her black eyes
gaze down: *We'll always*
have Paris, whether in Paris

or in pairs, but now, from where
I stand, *face to face*, here
is looking at you.

FLOURISH

It's the *fin de siècle*
before last, past
the lunar craze of the
Victorian age but before
the copper beech have given up
their leaves. Yew *broderie*,
hornbeam bosque, a hedged
allée of limbed-up trees:
the geese feeding beneath
must be stitching this world
to the next—*pied-à-terre*,
parterre, embroidery—the way
silk taffeta's held
close to a velvet drape
by the words *gold thread*.
Now geese hurry across
the sky like ballerinas, wings
flung back: *plissé*,
plié. If it were
travesty, a change of
dress, I'd call out *belong,*
dearest, lengthening of day,
May until summer: tarry,
linger, don't be
long: long reign, long
live.

SANS SERIF

It's the opposite of
Baroque, so I want
none of it—clean
and spare, like Cassius
it has that lean
and hungry look, Mercury's
clipped heels, the rag
of the body without
breath. A chorus of
alleluias, on the other
hand, is not only opulent
but copious, a cornucopia
of opinion which concludes
that opera is work, the *haute* gold
opus of the soprano, which does not
oppress yet presses against
her chest like the green glass *flacon*
de l'opéra held between
her breasts to keep the cognac
warm. Her notes hop
from hope to hope
like the layers of *l'opéra*
cake: Steeped in coffee syrup,
buttercream and *ganache* rising
in between, and a thin
chocolate coat slipped
over all, its name is scrolled
in glaze across the top—*l'opéra*
finished with a lick
of gold leaf.

"If We Never Meet Again"

after Keely Smith

In van Gogh's *View of the Sea*
at Scheveningen, a boat

sets off into a roiling sea, paint
thick with sand blown onto

the canvas from the beach
where van Gogh worked—not the same

as the sand we mixed into the paint
for the front porch steps to keep

from slipping in winter. Cicero tells how
Themistocles refused to learn

the art of memory, saying he preferred the science
of forgetting, but would Themistocles

believe the sand's no longer there, now that
the painting's been stolen? By winter

the rake had erased our entire
yard, grazing its Ouija board

of leaves, but did it ever spell
a ray cleaves to the highest point

of the shore, or just *rake*
leaves? Sure, there were embers

called *December* and *remember*, but did they
burn or sing—singe, rise,

combust like the ashes
of van Gogh's sea? After we left

The Hague, where did we stay
in Scheveningen? It was evening:

we went out to see the water, came
back in again—were we ever in

Scheveningen? It wasn't spring
but *come what May*, so if you can't

recall, decide whether you'd rather
remember spending hours

next to the sea, against
the sea, or in ecstasy.

STARLING,

it's all *a capella*, bright
northern sky in October,

and Jeroboam, Methuselah,
Salmanazar, and Balthazar wait

out in *la campagne*
riddling, keeping time

the way the French celebrate
birth by touching the lips

of a new baby with fine
champagne. *Go easy with*

delicacies thought: how *morbier*
keeps a thin layer of *ask*

between the morning and evening
milk, a horizon of ash below

the sky outside the chapel, no matter how
many syllables of alleluia

the soprano sings. All day long
the moon has thought

of her mushroom cap
which just now blooms

into view: you there,
at the world's waist, one hip

rising—you're the closest thing
to us; because of you,

under the maple the first fallen
stars still intend

to glow.

REQUIEM

Each October the house beyond
the woods appears, then goes away

in May. The maple opens
to let the blue jay in, then

closes, while all
the trees keep pointing

in the same direction.
Every house is

a missionary, claimed Frank Lloyd Wright,
but what is it they want

us to believe? Beside the house,
a road, and onto the road raccoon,

possum, ground hog, deer occasionally
stray: how the hind leg rises

at death, saluting
the sky, just as at the end

of Stravinsky's *Rite of*
Spring, a girl steps onto

the stage and dances herself
to death. The ground keeps opening

but will not speak. To attract
birds, you must make sounds

like a bird dying. Begin
with alarm—*pssshhtt*—then

move on to the high-pitched
noises small birds make

when seized by a predator: loudly
kiss the back of your hand

or thumb. The origin of music was
grief: a dirge sung annually

in memory of Linos, *ai Linon, alas for
Linos*, from the Phoenician *ai lanu, alas*

for us, a harvest
song, lament for the death

of the year. In October, as in Wagner,
you can have the gold

but only by renouncing
love, the past can sometimes be

forgotten, and heaven go up
in flames. Wagner always loved to be

where he died, in Venice,
because he could hear music

only in the city's silence.

ACCIDENTAL

Orient yourself, occasionally
fall down to the setting
sun, red dent in
the sky like a signature
in the key of
what? Scriabin thought
the musical note C was red;
Rimsky-Korsakov said A
is pink. Not planned
or foreseen, without warning
there's a sharp or flat, altered
note not belonging. Upside
down the goldfinches hang
like commas, like rest.
On occasion, remember
that in Venice there is
no dust, *non troppo*,
not too much, but if you must fall,
fall west: each evening, gather
in baskets the day lilies'
blooms, watch how they close
by the bushel.

CHEZ NOUS

                    we say *vive*
la différence between morals
and morels: the accent,
spelling, shape of the mouth
whenever it eats or
speaks. According to Sargent,
a portrait is a painting
with something wrong with
the mouth, but *chez nous*
the paintings have
no mouths and do not need
to sing because what we call
darkness darkens
in octaves.
               And indeed,
if we consider this beautiful
machine of the world,
Palladio wrote, so much needs
oiling: the porch swing
of the chickadee's song, the mourning
dove flung up like the window's
wooden sash, the word
rudbeckia.
                And isn't news
rude, the way
it beckons? *Le corps*
becomes a copse, someone's
opus, but we can't imagine
whose because *chez nous*
the peonies dress for dinner
like grizzlies

            in their pungent
fuchsia coats while the dead
settle back and go on
discussing how to leave
a world that begins
each April to finish
its sentence with another
inch of green.
            Let Marcus Aurelius go on
believing he has the last
say—you'd need to be stoic
to believe the universe
will be destroyed in a great
conflagration and then be re-formed
exactly as it was before. *Chez nous*
the world will end
like the end of Haydn's *Farewell*
Symphony, when all the players,
one by one, get up
from their seats and walk
offstage.

Rage Italic

So much happens
offstage, where the gods make

change—the Sphinx, for example, eating
the citizens of Thebes when they

cannot answer her riddle,
the Theban shepherd at the moment

he decides not to follow
orders. All those prophecies

issued from Delphi: is there a font
for what takes place

offstage? When it is emphatic,
in a foreign language, or when

it has an independent function within
the main text, *the sentence is printed*

in italics, but like the roulette wheel
in Reno, the truth is

what it turns out
to be, and belief

a bet we place,
like baseball cards clipped

with clothespins to the spokes
of our bikes, the patter

of birds in a stone
bath. *Pater Noster,*

give us a set, one size, one
face of, say, *rage*

italic, favorite font
of the gods. The Roman

courtesans had their sandals engraved
so that their footprints read

follow me, but to move
is always to bear

change, like all the moving
vans in Athens, *metaphor*

lettered on their sides. *Beware*
of Greeks bearing

change, some oracle must once
have said, because on the island

of Delos no one is allowed
to give birth or die. According to

history, what bears repeating is not
the same as what bears

repeating. From Old French, *font*
follows *fondre*, to melt

or cast, to found, to blend
or vanish. *What is here*

and not? The lost
and found, what's

italicized, *beurre Normande*,
what we never

mention, whatever will melt
in your mouth.

STILL LIFE

I like the pasta the way we
remember it, the Colosseum
as we meant it
to be: two Greek theaters
face to face. The past is always
hungry, but there is nothing tragic
in pasta, always filling
its plate so that the gods will at last
be satisfied and go away.

                        Quintillian describes
The Sacrifice of Iphigenia, how Timanthes
renders grief by veiling
Agamemnon's face, which he likens
rhetorically to the power
of silence. Longest heard,
the high-heeled woman at Fifth
& 83rd, sobbing beside the museum
of art—we didn't ask
what's wrong?

               One room was filled
with Vermeers, the scratching of crickets, and chirps
of paired birds, pressing
against a forest of ears. Can you hear
the *Woman in a Red Hat* looking
your way? She has just come from
Rome, has eaten *farfalle*
al burro, *pecorino* for lunch,
and the brushed red verb of
her hat has something
to say: *svaha*,
the time between

                    lightning
and thunder, the time spent
waiting for promises
to be fulfilled. She lives in the village
of Romancement, where Lewis Carroll longed
to stay, long after he realized
that the sign he passed on the
way out of town belonged
to the company named *ROMAN
CEMENT*.

NATURAL HISTORY

Pliny explained that ancient Rome
had two populations—those who breathed
and those who were made of stone,
each taking their place each day
at home, in palaces, theaters, piazzas, and baths—
and of the ones who remained in 1506
on the Esquiline Hill, *Laocoön*
was pulled from the earth
while Michelangelo and all the artists
who had gathered to see
began to draw, to speak
of how it was
too brief—the season
of peaches, arctic rose
nectarines, and statues rising
from the ground—but proof, nonetheless,
that the dead can be raised
in space chiseled
and nudged, chipped and dinged
by words (*half moon*,
mezzaluna, new moon, knife),
their lips first sealed then
parting, respite
then reprise, giving in, saying
when.

VILLA ROTONDA

A classic Ionic
portico rises above the hill,
and between its two columns could be entrance or

space with a wing stretching out on each side, rapture
headed your way. Intimate, divine,
Dante's *contrapasso*:

if on this side an arch,
on that side an arch, a *loggia* here,
a *loggia* there; a wing for a wing, an eye for

an eye—but what kind of a way to build villas
is that? Palladio believed that
pediments should admit,

that harmony can be
calculated by applying the
numerical equivalents of musical

harmonies to architectural space: a post-
and-lintel, contrapuntal love like
the scent of a lily

always pulling you to
the pistil of its throat. From above,
the villa looks like soliloquy, nothing but

stairways leading up to its face, and the mouth a
round hole at the center of four bare
rooms, cross hairs in the scope.

APOSTROPHE

How many in a field
of wheat, and to whom
do they belong? *O death, O*
grave, Bright star, thou bleeding piece
of earth, thou shouldst be
living at this hour, world without
synonym, amen. But I
digress, turn away like Giotto's
contrapposto Christ, apostle
of *contrecœur*—nothing like the cardinal
calling this morning, the third
fifty-degree day at the end
of December, to his cinnamon
mate. The headline says, "Pope Calls
Cardinals to Rome." But will they
come? It is written above—superscript, sign,
omission—*a gentle tender insinuation*
that makes it very difficult to definitely
decide to do without it. One does
do without it, I
do, I mostly always do, but
I cannot deny that from time
to time I feel myself
having regrets and from time to
time I put it in. This do in remembrance
of me, your only wick
to light. For where two
or three are gathered in
my name, like snow in April, lid
on a coffin, ice on the lake, I'll come
between you and yours; I give you
my word.

LE NON-DIT

How it apes the shape of
everything, steady in descent, quiet
as snow. Like Debussy's *La Plus Que
Lente*, it's more than slow and goes on
and on like the wind remembering
everywhere it has blown. *It's just after
this curve*, you say for the eighth
or ninth time, as we wind our way
up Skyline Drive into the Blue Ridge
mountains. Somewhere between
here and the top is the turn that might
take us back to the place that was
your home before your home
became the park, and in the time it takes
to reach the top and start
back down, you've gone back
through most of your favorites, hairpin
curves in the road: *The morning you were born,
the neighbors said they knew I'd gone
to the hospital because the snow hadn't been
swept from the coal box lid. Life goes on
with you or without. Now Christmas is just
as far away as it ever was. The folks up at Madison
catch wind of something and take it
like a sail. I'm a mother; I love
both my children the same. Nobody else's
blood but mine flows through
your veins. Even Jesus only had one
cross to bear. Ever since I was a child, I've loved
the snow. Someday I won't
be here, but you can look out at the snow
and think of me.*

PATTOU'S FRENCH-ENGLISH MANUAL

for the use of Physicians, Nurses, Ambulance-Drivers and Workers in Civilian Relief, 1917

1. Hello there, stretcher-bearers! Turn out!
11. Here we are in the trench.
12. *Quel spectacle!*
27. *Est-ce grave?*
28. Yes, he is severely wounded in the abdomen and head. He is riddled with bullets.
29. *Il agonise. Il est mort.*
30. What is the matter, my friend?
43. Driver, be very careful. Go slowly. The road is full of ruts.
44. *Ça secoure les blessés d'une façon terrible.*
44. It shakes the wounded terribly.
51. *Adieu! Bonne chance!*

Pronunciation Helps

a—is usually long	As in English words like father, bar. Exemplified by *âge, entrant.*
a—is sometimes short	As in English words like bat. Exemplified in *mal.*
è—with *accent grave*	As in English words like e'er, there. Exemplified in *père, mère.*
é—with *accent aigu*	As in English words like air.
i—	As in English words like seek, me, sea. Exemplified in *pique, étourdi.*
î—	As in English words like field. Exemplified in *gîte.*

o—   As in English words like sob.
                           Exemplified in *sol*.
ô—   As in English words like no.

6.   He is opening his eyes. No, he has stopped breathing.
      It is the end.
8.   The poor boy, he is dead. What is his name?
9.   *Voici sa plaque d'identité.*

The *liaison* is the sounding of the final consonant of a word,
thus connecting it with a succeeding word which begins with
a vowel or h mute.

16.   Open the mouth wide, my brave fellow.
17.   *Respirez fortement. Faites "Ah!"*
32.   Do you like music? I am mad about music.
56.   Write us from time to time and give us your news.
57.   Please accept a little remembrance, nurse.

7.   Show me your tongue, please.
17.   Would you like to hear the phonograph play, (sir)? Do
      you prefer a classical air or something popular?
18.   Play me "Since the Day" from the opera *Louise.* I adore
      it.

5.   *Êtes-vous d'ici?*
5.   Do you live around here?
6.   *Êtes-vous du pays?*
6.   Are you from this part of the country?
14.   Can one drink the water in the well over there?
15.   Here is a pail and a tin cup.
16.   It is forbidden to drink that water.
17.   It is very good.

The verb *aller* is used idiomatically in many useful ways. *Aller*, to go; to be (well, or ill); to form future tense (with infinitive) of any verb desired.

EX. *Je vais mal.* I am ill. *Je vais boire.* I am going to drink.

36.   *Vous allez vous remettre.*
36.   You are going to get well.
41.   Fortunately you are better than you were yesterday.
42.   I dread the change.

12.   *Qu'y-a-t-il de nouveau ce matin?*
12.   What is the news this morning?
15.   Do you want me to write a letter to your family?
16.   *Voulez-vous écrire vous-même?*
16.   Do you want to write yourself?
21.   I am sorry that I speak French so badly.
22.   *J'ai du mal à me faire comprendre.*
22.   I have trouble to make myself understood.
23.   You flatter me. I studied French as a child.
27.   *En été. En automne. En hiver* [ee-vair]. *Au printemps.*
27.   In summer. In the autumn. In the winter. In the spring. (Note variation.)

Exemplified by *été, charmé, donné.*

The letter x is pronounced (like an s) if it is the final consonant in a word standing alone. The others are silent when standing alone or in a word terminating a sentence.

EX.   *Elle a dix* [deese] *enfants.* She has ten children.
       Elle a dix [dee] *francs.* She has ten francs.
       Elle en a dix [deese]. She has ten (of them).
       Vous allez [aleze] *à New-York.* You are going to New York.
       Vous allez [allay] *rester chez-vous.* You are going to remain at home.

MADAME X

after John Singer Sargent

What I've been
missing all these years
has little to do with
sin, nothing to do
with tax, just black
and white like the seasons
in Antarctica, either day
or night. For two months
of winter dark, the Emperor
Penguin stands in the coldest
place on earth, holding
one egg on top of its
feet, inches above
the ice, just as the bodice of the black
satin dress keeps holding Madame
X and the wolf's head lifted
in her thighs. Even the gown is missing
a strap, but not missing it sincerely
since one shoulder basks,
unkissed: the word *glacier*
before it's pronounced.
What if you call a spade
a spade? The sharp, flat
blade of the body turns
upside down and looks
like a heart cupping the edge
of where a heart would be
in a future so tense, its tents pitch
on the sea without your having

to ask, like sin with no consequence,
the mouth just opening
its lips, before syntax.

SHOCKING

like all the light and the birds
and the fish in the world
put together, it is *a color*
of China and Peru but not of
the West: violent magenta, hot
hot pink, the color
Schiaparelli first viewed
from her baby carriage, parked
among the begonias. *Since most women*
do not know themselves, she said, *they should try*
to do so: search the shops of Paris
for a slip, a bra, panties
in the color the French still call
le shocking, or make a voyage
to Begonia—country in which to be
and be gone are one, country of name
that tune while it's still
being played—and send back the address
of gold *lamé*, *vermeil*, border
between body and dress. *Choc*,
from *choquer*—to strike with fear—
shocking, how many ways
to get to a woman's body: *la jupe*
culotte, carving the space between
her thighs, "Lightning Fasteners"
unzipped from waist to hip, and—the year
before Hitler invaded Poland—a white sheath
Schiaparelli designed with wounds
to resemble torn flesh: silk crepe skin
slashed and pulled back to the magenta
beneath, pink and black fur hanging

like tongues. *Never fit a dress to*
the body, but train the body
to fit the dress: for the summer
of 1939 she shaped a bustle gown of
satin printed with Mae West
walking a poodle, her silhouette identical
to that of the dress. In the last spring
before the war, for her *Commedia dell'arte*
collection, among the masks
and gloves, Schiaparelli designed
a wasp-waist, full-length evening
coat in a harlequin pattern of light
flicked from the tail fins of fish and
the wings of birds unfurled, waving
to the world: red, white, yellow,
blue, and black hourglasses,
all of them full.

ENSEMBLE

La Maison Worth
Advertisement for the House of Worth,
by Paul Reboux, circa 1920

*Le printemps, qui réjouit les cœurs humains,
réalise chaque année une sorte de miracle.
D'un arbre robuste, enraciné profondément,
d'un chêne royal qui domine une forêt tout
entière, il fait naître des bourgeons sensibles,
des feuilles fraîches, un foisonnement de
verdure qui palpite et s'émeut aux plus légers
souffles de l'air nouveau.*

*La Maison Worth a quelque chose de
cette destinée à la fois auguste et souriante.*

*On peut affirmer que, si certains hommes
achètent un titre de noblesse à Rome, toutes
les femmes, en portant une robe de chez
Worth, s'honorent d'un brevet d'élégance,
de style et de bonne tenue.*

*C'est le résultat d'une ancienne renommée.
Pourtant, cette renommée, on n'y songe
guère, en visitant cette maison bruissante
d'une vie multiple. Bien qu'elle soit affermie
et comme enracinée par ses traditions de
grande classe, chaque saison s'y manifeste
avec élan par des créations d'une audace
harmonieuse. Elle est sensible aux moindres
innovations de la mode. Elle est pleine d'une
jeunesse plus émouvante encore que celle
des forêts d'avril: la jeunesse parisienne.*

The House of Worth

translation of Paul Reboux's advertisement

Spring, which delights the human heart,
realizes each year a kind of miracle.
From a robust tree, deeply rooted,
from a regal oak that towers above
an entire forest, it arouses buds
so that they bring forth new leaves,
a profusion of greenery that flutters and stirs
in the lightest breaths of new air.

The House of Worth has something
of this destiny at once august and smiling.

It can be said that if some men
purchase a title of nobility from Rome, all
women, in wearing a dress of Worth,
honor themselves with a certificate of elegance,
style and good manners.

This is the result of a time-honored reputation.
Yet, visiting this venerable institution—which teems
with such varied life—one scarcely imagines
this renown. Though indeed strengthened
and firmly rooted by traditions of great
distinction, here each new season is expressed
in a passionate surge of daring, harmonious
creations. House or woman, she is sensitive
to the slightest innovations of fashion. She is full of
a youthfulness more stirring still than that
of the woods in April: Parisian youth.

May Some Word

Lip-printed alms! The key to rejoicing lay in the human curse,
really shocking to any who sought the mere lack
done to our racing bust, profound as a mount
but dungeon *royale* to *Domine*, who forgets to
enter entirely, ill-fated *maître d'* of bourgeoning eons
without syllables, days fully fresh and forgotten,
where the key palpates and smooches, only proving lingerie
swoops deliriously low.

May some word question those, decent destiny, who
opted for *foie gras* at your surreal aunt's in August:

one pure affirming curtsy, certain hums—
ah, so taunting—the noblest aroma. Two
lay famished, important to one robed in the shape
of a word, sonorant end of brevity, elegant
like steel—and debonair, too.

Say the reigning sultan of ancient doom
pours tons of this rain on me, any song—air
invisible at the onset—may soon breeze or ante up
dunes of envy, multi-lipped. This being the case, why offer me
a calm in raw *c*'s and *a*'s, on a par, say, with a tray of tea on
ground glass? Jacques says one seems festive
if a land party craves tea on the dunes or dashes after
harmony on the loose. Elysian Fields won't mind,
I know, if I have tea on Limoges or a model airplane
of doom: June has proved a moving encore for your aunt to sell
the forest of the real and let June's nest pair *e*'s in the end.

ON YELLOWED VELVET

> Sur du velours jauni, *performance*
> *direction from Satie's* Danse Maigre

At ease on the lawn, the sacrificial
deer stand adjacent to the statue
of St. Francis. They are slower than
adagio, than the Basilica
of Assisi with its ceremonial
rights, but sacred and holy like the face
of the ocean, neither below
nor above. And there's nothing
artificial about them; they stand and stand
for what touches both *don't*
and *know*. What's uncanny,
unheimlich, in German is not
heimlich, secret, and certainly not *heim*,
home, which means home can't be
where the heart is but the Hôtel
Tassel in Brussels, whose staircases
turn and let down their lips
to meet you, whips unfurling
like vines. Freud said we'll know
the uncanny when surprised
by some *heimlich*, some fear or
desire we've repressed
come home, pressing
the shore like the ocean's thin
lips as they sink
into sand. What's left
when the white-tailed deer have
disappeared in the woods will be

cloven, heart-shaped
tracks. While you sit writing
at your *bonheur du jour*, the woods fill
with accent trees or, if
you prefer, eccentricities.

A History of Reality

Taken literally, the shore would be
littoral and the ocean its Latin
lover *litura*, erasure or
correction, clearing the beach
like a windshield with its big
glassy hands. Waving, yes,
but to whom? It's morning already
and all the world's a mess or else
at Mass. *Each matin bell,*
the Baron saith,/ Knells us back
to a world of death, but *was für*
Wetter gibt es heute? What kind of
weather is it giving today? Not *The Sorrows*
of Young Werther, I hope. Snowflakes begin
x-ing out the [   ] *y*: signs, ciphers, sighs
the size of cygnets. Later
on, the weather turns
over and considers whether, after
the matinee, *litura* and
the shore will go on
keeping time, those hands
gripping the place a waist
would be if an hour
had one, applauding
their shadow-puppet
swan, their own
signature song.

IN VOGUE

A lock of hair turns
in its locket, curled in the imperfect
tense because it must speak
of what happens again
and again, like the recurring
dream of Henri Sauguet in which
he met up with Satie in
heaven and Satie whispered
in his ear: *Tell me, my friend,*
do they still think I'm
dead, down there? Perdu
can mean both lost
and wasted, although *pain*
perdu is neither, and what's
in *vogue* is what continues
to row in waves across
the ocean, like mourners
singing in rounds:

When the roll . . . . is called up yon - - - - - - - - der, When the
    When the roll is called up yonder, I'll be there,

roll . . . . . . is called up yon - - - - - - der, When the roll . . . . is called up
 When the roll is called up yonder, I'll be there,   *When the roll is called up*

yonder, When the roll is called up yonder, I'll be there.

According to the Gregorian Sacramentary, our names are written
in the Book of Life and we are
dedicated to God because he writes
his law in our hearts. So at the dedication

of a church, the bishop writes from corner
to corner across the floor of the
basilica; with the point
of his staff, he inscribes
two alphabets—one in Greek, the other
in Latin—along two lines of
ashes laid out in the form
of an X. After hearing Maria
Callas as Medea, Franco Zeffirelli
divided history into B.C.
and A.C.—Before
Callas and After—but when
her ashes were scattered over
the ship's railing to the sea,
a sudden gust sent them
back into the faces
of those on board.

PALINODE

In lieu of song, *liaison*:
let the usually silent, final
consonant of a word be pronounced
when followed by a word
beginning with a vowel, and pour out
the sentiment left at the bottom
of the glass when I've finished
the *Beaune-Grèves Vigne de
l'Enfant Jésus*, claimed by the nuns
who once owned the vineyard to produce
wine as smooth as the Baby Jesus
in velvet pants. I meant
sediment, suspension not so much
willing as not disbelieved. *Blest
be the ties that bind*, the ties
that won't. So that's settled: let words
be the Montmorency cherries I bought
at market because the woman pronounced them
Mount Mercy, let them be the tumult
of memory, mute.

DANCE OF ANCIENT KNOSSOS

after Satie's Gnossienes

Build a palace at Knossos, a labyrinth
from which there is no
escape, if you want to hear the sound
of the past, although there will be
no sound—only the home that once
held it like Satie's framed mirror
he moved to each new
place because it was "laden
with memories."

                             With the tip of your thought. Postulate
within yourself. Step by
                  step. On the tongue.

And keep time
at the palace of *gnosis*, knowledge; let it lean
back like recognition, legs crossing over
and over while an *ostinato* bass
holds like stones beneath a current
of notes.

                     Slow. Advise yourself carefully. Arm yourself
with clairvoyance. Alone for an instant. So that you obtain
                  a hollow.

The river chants, looks
like a thread you could
follow—incantation without motif, "music
on one's knees," a Greek
dance performed right to
left, then left
to right, then stationary
before an altar:

Very lost. Carry that further. Open your head. Bury the sound.

NOTES

Dedication: Gertrude Stein, "Poetry and Grammar."
Epigraphs: Edith Wharton, "The Fullness of Life"; Theodor
    Adorno, *Minima Moralia*.

"Portrait": Stéphane Mallarmé, "Prose (*pour des Esseintes*)."
"*Chère Personne*": Noel Arnaud, *L'état d'ébauche*.
"Starling,": "Go easy with delicacies thought," www.fran-
    toiodisommaia.it
"Apostrophe": Gertrude Stein, "Poetry and Grammar."
"Shocking": Elsa Schiaparelli, "Twelve Commandments for
    Women." *Shocking Life* (1954); Dilys E. Blum, *Shock-
    ing! The Art and Fashion of Elsa Schiaparelli* (2003);
    Judith Thurman, "Mother of Invention," *The New
    Yorker* (October 27, 2003). Plastic zippers called
    "Lightening Fasteners" were introduced in 1932 by
    the Lightening Fastener Company of Great Britain.
"A History of Reality": Samuel Taylor Coleridge, "Christa-
    bel," Part II.
"In Vogue": *Songs of Faith* (1933).
"Palinode": O. V. de Milosz, *Amoureuse initiation*; Jay McIner-
    ney, "Uncorked," *House & Garden* (May 2001).
"Dance of Ancient Knossos": The italicized lines are perfor-
    mance directions from Erik Satie's *Gnossienne #1* and
    #3. Gymnopédies, Gnossiennes and Other Works for Piano
    (Dover 1989).

ACKNOWLEDGMENTS

Thanks to the editors of the following journals in which some of these poems first appeared:

The Antioch Review: "A History of Reality," "Apostrophe"
Barrow Street: "*Chère Personne*"
Boston Review: "Requiem"
Chautauqua Literary Journal: "Proverbs," "*Rendez-Vous*"
The Cincinnati Review: "Flourish," "'If We Never Meet Again,'" "Portrait," "Ensemble"
FIELD: "*Chez Nous*," "Elegy," "On Yellowed Velvet," "Paramour"
Green Mountains Review: "Kind of Blue," "Rage Italic," "*Sans Serif*"
Inkwell: "Shocking," "*Amuse-Bouche*"
Lake Effect: "Palinode"
The Laurel Review: "Accidental," "In Vogue"
Los Angeles Review: "*Madame X*"
Mid-American Review: "Natural History," "Starling," "*Vis-à-Vis*"
Ninth Letter: "Dance of Ancient Knossos"
The Paris Review: "Villa Rotonda"
Pleiades: "Cadenza"
Ploughshares: "*Badinerie*"
Slate: "True Confessions"
Sou'wester: "Still Life"

"A History of Reality" also appeared on *Poetry Daily*; "Kind of Blue" and "Proverbs" also appeared on *Verse Daily*.

My gratitude to all of my editors at Oberlin, and special thanks to Martha Collins, who read this manuscript in many places, many forms. Thanks to the Ohio Arts Council for their support.

About the Author

Angie Estes is the author of two previous collections of poems, *The Uses of Passion* and *Voice-Over*, winner of the 2001 FIELD Poetry Prize and the 2001 Alice Fay Di Castagnola Award from the Poetry Society of America.

A Note on the Type

The text of this book was set in Bembo. Bembo was modeled on typefaces cut by Francesco Griffo for Aldus Manutius' printing of *De Aetna* in 1495 in Venice, a book by the Renaissance writer and humanist scholar Pietro Bembo about his visit to Mount Etna. Griffo's design is considered one of the first of the old style typefaces that were used as staple text types in Europe for 200 years. The italic is modeled on the handwriting of the Renaissance scribe Giovanni Tagliente.